Conflict Resolution Through Literature

"Romeo and Juliet"
Curriculum Unit

By Barbara Marderosian, *M.Ed., J.D.*

RoseDog Books

PITTSBURGH, PENNSYLVANIA 15222

ISBN-10: 0-8059-8860-2
ISBN-13: 978-0-8059-8860-4

Printed in the United States of America

First Printing

For information or to order additional books, please write:
RoseDog Books
701 Smithfield St.
Third Floor
Pittsburgh, PA 15222
U.S.A.
1-800-834-1803
Or visit our web site and
on-line bookstore at www..rosedogbookstore.com

Foreword

Conflict is a part of every day life and can be viewed as an opportunity for growth rather than as an occasion to despair. Characters in literature face conflicts great and small. Many of the issues confronted are relevant to students' lives and therefore can be used to make literature more relevant. In addition to prompting students' discussion and composition, the objective of this curriculum unit is to provide a vehicle through which the concepts of mediation can be introduced by teachers to complement what they teach already on a regular basis.

Content Overview

Shakespeare's Biography

Plot Summary

Definition of Mediation

General Objectives for Each Act

Glossary for Each Act

Principal Conflict and Questions for Each Act

Focus Mediation Skills for Each Act

Extended Activities for Each Act

Quizzes for Each Act

Assessments for the Work as a Whole

About the Author

Dr. Barbara A. Marderosian is a long-time Massachusetts public school educator who has worked in both urban and rural settings primarily with high school English classes. She is a graduate of New England School of Law and is certified in mediation which she practices privately and in conjunction with the Worcester Community Mediation Center.

The Life of Wm. Shakespeare
Essential Facts:

• Shakespeare was born in Stratford-upon-Avon in 1564 and died in 1616.

• His parents were John and Mary (Arden) Shakespeare.

• He married Anne Hathaway when she was 26 and he 18.

• They had three children: Susanna, and twins Hamnet and Judith.

• It is unknown exactly how he entered the theatre world of London.

• "Romeo and Juliet" was written c. 1594, one of his early tragedies.

• His plays can be broken down into primarily three groups: tragedies, comedies, and histories.

• He also is known for composing the English sonnet form.

• The theatre with which he is most commonly associated is "the Globe."

• The Globe Theatre was a wooden, octagonal, open-air theatre.

• Women were not allowed to act during Elizabethan times.

• Most of his plays follow the following five act format:
  1. the exposition
  2. the rising action
  3. the climax
  4. the falling action
  5. the denouement

• Lord Chamberlain was Shakespeare's patron from c. 1594-1603.

• King James I served as his primary patron after that.

• "Hamlet" is considered Shakespeare's masterpiece.

General Plot Summary

Act I – The Exposition

The purpose of an exposition is to introduce the readers/audience members to the principal characters. The play opens with a street brawl between servants of the Montagues and of the Capulets, two prominent households in the city of Verona, Italy. Though the feud between these two families is apparently a longstanding one, the origin of it is never explained. At one point, the hot-headed Tybalt, a nephew of Capulet, and Benvolio, a Montague, have a sword fight. Because the two families have caused so much unrest, Prince Escalus issues a decree stating that the next to initiate a fight will be condemned to death. Afterwards, Romeo enters. He is distracted because his love Rosaline is not interested in him. Romeo's friends Benvolio and Mercutio are going to a party held by the Capulets. Though they are not invited, they are not concerned that their identities will be discovered since it is a masque, similar to a costume party. In fact, their primary motivation for going is to cheer the lovesick Romeo and show him that there are other eligible women in the city. Meanwhile Juliet, the only daughter of Capulet, learns before the party that her father wishes her to marry the wealthy Count Paris. Though Capulet is concerned that Juliet is a bit young (not quite 13), both her mother and Nurse think she is of marrying age. Juliet agrees to consider it. However, instead of looking upon Paris at the party, she meets Romeo and the two fall instantly in love before they even know one another's last names. Before they have time to do so, Tybalt recognizes Romeo and wants to fight. His uncle stops him. Afterwards, Juliet learns Romeo's last name and is shocked to learn that he is of the Montague family.

Act II – The Rising Action

The rising action in a play is caused by a plot twist. In Act II, the readers learn that later that night, Romeo climbs into the Capulet orchard and speaks to Juliet who is out on her balcony. They make plans to secretly wed. Through the Nurse, Romeo gets word to Juliet to meet him at Friar Laurence's chamber. Friar Laurence weds the two in hopes that it will heal the rift between the opposing families.

Conflict Resolution Through Literature

Act III – The Climax

The climax contains the turning point of the story. Immediately after the two are married, Romeo is walking down the street and finds Mercutio and Tybalt in a heated exchange. Romeo tries to break up the fight but succeeds in getting in the way and blocking Mercutio's view. Mercutio is stabbed under Romeo's arm and dies. Romeo becomes enraged and slays Tybalt. Romeo runs away because he has killed Tybalt on pain of death. Juliet later finds out that Romeo has killed her cousin but decides to stay true to her new husband regardless. Once Escalus hears of the events, he mercifully alters the punishment to banishment instead of death. Romeo is very upset because this means he will be away from Juliet. Meanwhile, the Capulets pressure Juliet about marrying Paris.

Act IV- The Falling Action

The falling action explains how the plot unfolds, leading up to the tragic conclusion. Friar Laurence comes up with a plan he believes will help Romeo and Juliet. He gives Juliet a potion that will make her appear dead after she drinks it but in reality, she'll be asleep. After she is placed in the tomb, she will wake up. In the meantime, Friar Laurence will get word to Romeo who is now in the city of Mantua. He will return for Juliet and the two can leave together to continue their lives. Juliet agrees to the plan and does execute it. Her parents, the Nurse, and Paris are greatly saddened when they believe she is dead.

Act V – The Denouement

The denouement, or conclusion, comes when Balthasar, a servant of the Montagues, mistakenly informs Romeo of Juliet's death. Friar Laurence's letter explaining the ruse never reaches Romeo. Romeo is distraught and buys poison before returning secretly to the Capulets' tomb. There, he sees the sleeping Juliet, and mourns her "death." He drinks the poison and dies. Juliet awakes, sees Romeo dead, and kills herself. When the tragic outcome is discovered, the Capulets and Montagues learn of the couple's love through Friar Laurence. It takes this great loss for them to stop the feud once and for all.

Mediation Definition
Process Overview

There are various types and styles of conflict resolution; mediation is one of them. The purpose of this overview is to explain the goals of facilitative mediation. Mediation is a **process** in which disputants can reach peaceful resolution. Mediators facilitate **communication** to that end by allowing participants to vent their concerns, and focus on sorting out underlying issues and feelings. The role of mediator is not to side with one party or the other, but to remain **neutral.** Mediators are often helpful in asking **open-ended questions** after carefully listening to both parties' concerns. Some helpful ones are – How would you like to see this resolved?; What might happen if this is not resolved?; What was it like before the conflict began? Though there are different approaches to the mediation process, the following structure is a useful one:

Opening Remarks – the mediator explains his/her role and the goal of mediation

Step 1 – Select one disputant at random and allow him/her to explain his concerns while the other disputant listens. The other party may not interrupt but can jot down questions or concerns to be addressed later. The mediator should actively listen and sum up after the party is done. If the mediator needs to ask questions for the purpose of clarifying information, it should be done at this time. Do not judge. Do not give advice. Just listen and gather information. Take notes as needed. After a mediator is sure that all concerns have been vented, it is time for the next party to do the same.

Step 2 – The second disputant now has a turn. The mediator should apply the same principals as above. Also, listen for any underlying issues/feelings that are not being expressed verbally but may be hinted at through tone of voice and body language.

Joint Session – Now explore ways in which things might be resolved. If there is more than one issue, break these down into small steps. Do a reality check and have disputants think of the consequences that might befall them if things remain the same. This might take some time.

The Agreement – Have the mediator sum up the terms of the agreement before putting them in writing. Try to write in a balanced fashion, i.e., explain what both parties' responsibilities are. After completion, have both parties and the mediator sign a written agreement.

OBJECTIVES Act I

• Students can identify examples of diction and tone on a target audience.

• Students can identify examples of non-verbal communication on a target audience.

• Students can identify the effects of diction and tone on a target audience.

• Students can identify the effects of non-verbal communication on a target audience.

• Students can identify typical human responses to conflict such as fear, anger, confrontation, denial, and consensus building.

GLOSSARY Act I

Active listening – reflecting back the speaker's related information

Character Foil – a character who enhances the traits of another by comparison

Diction – word choice

Nonverbal communication – body language that implies meaning

Tone – speaker's attitude toward his/her subject matter

Participation Rubric

A great deal of the **focus mediation skills** will be taught through class participation methods, specifically role play. The following assessment tool may be used periodically throughout the unit after activities and role plays to determine levels of participation and to provide feedback. Simply check the box which applies for formative assessment. Also, teachers who need summative grades that correspond with traditional marking may equate categories with corresponding letter or numerical grades, i.e., Advanced is equal to A/95; Proficient is equal to B/85; Developing is equal to C/75; and Beginning is D/65.

Benchmark- Effective Mediation – Student effectively mediates and employs skills thereof in a role-play situations.

Focus Mediation Skill:	Identifying Nonverbal Communication	Identifying Feelings	Active Listening	Asking Open-Ended Questions
Advanced	Student consistently and accurately interprets signs of nonverbal communication	Student consistently and accurately identifies feelings of a disputant	Student reflects back information to disputants accurately and consistently	Student consistently asks open-ended questions
Proficient	Student sufficiently interprets signs of non-verbal communication	Student sufficiently identifies feelings of a disputant	Student reflect back information to disputants frequently	Student frequently asks open-ended questions
Developing	Student occasionally identifies and interprets signs of non-verbal communication	Student occasionally identifies feelings of a disputant	Student reflects back information to disputants occasionally	Student occasionally asks open-ended questions occasionally
Novice	Student rarely identifies and interprets signs of non-verbal communication	Student rarely identifies feelings of a disputant	Student reflects back information to disputants rarely	Student rarely asks open-ended questions

"ROMEO AND JULIET"
Act I

Principal Conflict #1

In Act I, scene 1 of the play, the audience learns of a longstanding feud between the Montagues and the Capulets. Some of the servants of each house meet on the streets and instigate one another through both verbal and nonverbal communication.

Questions for Discussion or Composition:

What comments are made by the opposing parties which lead to the conflict?

What behaviors are exhibited by the opposing parties which lead to the conflict?

What dynamics occurring in scene 1 are similar to those you have witnessed firsthand when people you know are in conflict?

What might make it easier for people in a group to taunt one another rather than doing so as individuals?

Which character is the most hot-tempered in your opinion and how can the reader discern this?

Why do the citizens of Verona want to "beat down" the members of both families?

If you were in Prince Escalus's position, how would you handle the public brawl?

Focus Mediation Skills
Act I

Identifying Nonverbal Communication Skills

Step One: People often think of communication merely as the exchange of the spoken word. However, it is much more than that. Nonverbal communication, such as the use of gestures or facial expressions, often tells the onlooker more than words can. In order for students to practice the skill of correctly identifying emotions conveyed in this manner, give the rows in the class a slip of paper with an emotion written on it to be expressed without using words. Have the other members of the class try to identify the emotion and explain how they arrived at this conclusion.

Anger –

Sadness –

Frustration-

Joy –

Relief –

Step Two: Next, have students reread the opening scene of the play and identify two examples of nonverbal communication and the effect on its target audience.

Focus Mediations Skills
Act I Continued

Tone

Step One: Often times, the way something is said can be more important that what is literally stated. This activity will require one person from each of the rows to read the same statement, but with a different tone that changes the meaning. The statement is:

"He went to the movies with her last night."

Happy –

Sad –

Relieved –

Surprised –

Mocking –

Again, have onlookers determine the tone behind the statement and discuss how inflection and emphasis can change this one statement's meaning depending on the attitude of the speaker.

Step Two: Have the students go back through the opening scene of the play and discuss the tone that a Shakespearean actor would have used in delivering some of the lines leading up to the street brawl. Discuss the effects of diction used particularly by the characters Samson and Gregory. What words/phrases in particular are inflammatory and why?

Extended Activities

A. First, have students identify how the Act I characters respond verbally and non-verbally when they are in conflict. Then, have them list or demonstrate some of the things that students do or say when in conflict. Share these with a partner. Partners need to come up with at least one better way that his/her peer could deal with conflict. Students should report back to the class.

B. Have students research related topics such as gangs, mob psychology, and peer pressure. Are any of the dynamics manifested by the characters in the play similar to those identified in their research? If so, what are they? What insight does this information shed on characters' motivations?

C. Either photocopy the web diagram below or have students draw the it in their notebooks and fill in the blanks regarding some possible reactions that students might have if they were facing a similar type of conflict (breakout of a fight) in the hallway. (Some responses might include: run away, fight back, negotiate, notify the principal).

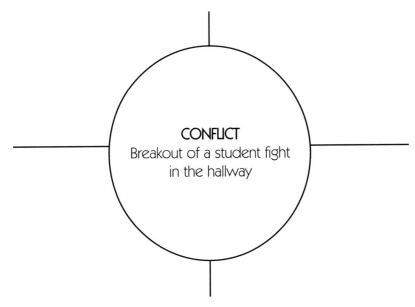

Dealing With Conflict QUIZ

Directions: Respond to the following questions in full sentences explaining your rationale (20 points each):

1. Who is the most at fault for the brawl in scene 1 and why?

2. Which character first tries to mediate and what are the results?

3. Compare and contrast the personality traits of Benvolio and Tybalt in one paragraph.

4. If you were directing this play, which contemporary actors would you select for **two** of the following roles and why?

A. Benvolio

B. Tybalt

C. Prince Escalus

D. Montague

E. Capulet

OBJECTIVES Act II

• Students can explain the concept of theme.

• Students can apply literary themes to "Romeo and Juliet."

• Students can identify principal conflicts in the play and the underlying feelings of main characters.

• Students should identify ways in which methods conflicts could be resolved.

GLOSSARY Act II

Catharsis – an emotional release or purging through art or literature

Characterization – the way in which an author provides details to the reader about characters in a literary work

Direct characterization – information provided by the author in the text i.e., "John is tall."

Indirect characterization – information that the reader can infer i.e., "John is captain of the basketball team." Inferences can be made from what a character says or does, or by what others say about him/her. *However, one cannot always assume this information to be correct without adequate textural evidence. Likewise, mediators should not make assumptions but ask questions to clarify anything that might be an assumption on their part or another party's part.

Theme – the central idea of a literary work

"ROMEO AND JULIET"
Act II

Principal Conflict #2

In Act I, scene 2 of the play, Romeo is introduced. He is in conflict with himself and his feelings of unrequited love for Rosaline. He also is conflicted, as is Juliet, when they fall in love but realize too late, that they are members of feuding families. In Act II, they agree to marry. Some of the most common themes in literature are the "man versus X" themes. The word versus implies conflict. There are many ways conflict is exhibited in a person/character. The themes illustrate this. Teachers should first identify and explain said themes. They are:

• Man vs. himself
• Man vs. man
• Man vs. society
• Man vs. nature
• Man vs. God
• Man vs. machine

Questions for Discussion or Composition:

Which themes are most prevalent in Act II? How are they illustrated?

If you were Romeo's counselor, what advice would you give him?

If you were Juliet's counselor, what advice would you give her?

What alternatives exist for Friar Laurence, other than marrying the couple? What might be the best option?

How does the concept of passion vs. reason operate in the play thus far?

What issues and feelings are still exhibited in the social world of today's teenager?

Conflict Resolution Through Literature

Focus Mediations Skills
Act II

Identifying Feelings

To be a good listener, one must be able to identify the feelings that motivate people's statements as well as understand the content of said statements.

Step One: Read the statements below and list at least two feelings that are expressed.

Student Says: **Student Feels:**

"I'm never going to have time to study after the game. I have to work and my boss will kill me if I'm late again."

"I didn't want to go to that dance anyway. It's for losers."

"I guess I'll talk to my counselor about it but I wish my dad would listen."

"If she doesn't stop talking about me, I'm going to kill her. I can't believe she used to be my best friend."

"What do you mean I failed the test! I studied for hours! Nobody is that stupid!"

Step Two: Reread the following excerpts from the play and identify the feelings expressed.

Character Says: **Character Feels:**

"O Romeo, Romeo, wherefore art thou Romeo? / Deny thy father and refuse thy name!"

                        -Juliet 2.2.33

"Young Son, it argues a distempered head/ So soon to bid good morrow to thy bed."

                        -Friar Laurence 2.3.33-34

"When and where and how/We met, we wooed, and and made exchange of vow/I'll tell thee as we pass; but this I pray, That thou consent to marry us today."

                        -Romeo 2.3.61-64

"Where the devil should this Romeo be? Came he not home tonight?"

                        -Mercutio 2.4.1

"Scurvy knave! Pray you, sir, a word…"

                        -Nurse 2.4.159

Conflict Resolution Through Literature

Teacher's Notes

Though answers may vary for the Feelings Exercises, below are some possible responses.

Step One/Student Feels...

- frustrated, concerned, pressured

- hurt, jealous

- despondent, isolated

- angry, hurt, spiteful

- frustrated, lacking self-esteem, unintelligent

Step Two/Character Feels...

- frustrated, rebellious

- concerned, miffed

- jubilant, impatient

- angry, protective

- irritated, overprotective

Extended Activities

A. Have students complete the Venn Diagram below comparing Tybalt and Benvolio. Discuss how these characters are different and how they are similar in personality and how this affects how they deal with conflict.

Tybalt   Commonalities   Benvolio

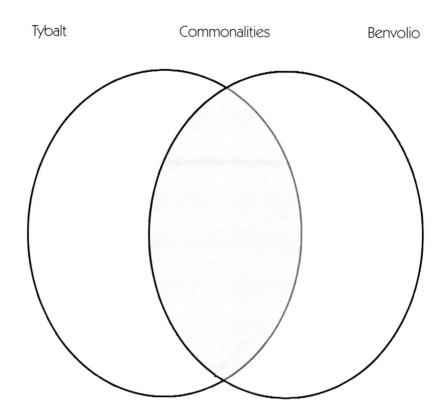

B. The way people deal with conflict is often affected by underlying emotions and attitudes. Examine the character of the Nurse. What feelings does she possess about Juliet? How can one infer this? How might the Nurse's attitudes affect her interactions with the following characters?

• Juliet
• Romeo
• Tybalt
• The Capulets

C. Humor can be a double-edged sword. Often, it diffuses conflict. Other times, it increases tension. Find specific examples from the text which illustrate both of these cases.

D. Assign each row in class one of the following characters and have them respond to the questions below:

Tybalt
Benvolio
Mercutio
Romeo
Juliet
Nurse

How would your character act if he/she attended your school? To what groups might he/she belong? To what cliques, if any? In what activities might he/she engage? Describe the contents of his/her locker? Would this character likely be your friend? Explain.

Dealing With Conflict QUIZ

Directions: Respond to the following questions in complete sentences explaining your rationale (20 points each):

1. Which character is the most loyal friend to Romeo? Defend your position.

2. What effect does the Nurse's stalling tactics have on Juliet?

3. How might the parents of Romeo and Juliet react if they were to discover the two are in love?

4. Romeo and Juliet are not in love, but just infatuated with one another. Defend or refute this statement.

5. Sometimes art can be a form of **catharsis** – a way of purging emotions. Draw a vignette for this chapter in the space provided below. Explain its relevance to plot events.

OBJECTIVES Act III

• Students can identify the turning point of the play.

• Students can articulate connections between conflicts in the play and conflicts in life.

• Students can articulate relevance between literature and life.

• Students can define pertinent literary devices.

• Students can identify literary devices in text.

• Students can explain how figures of speech affect communication between parties.

GLOSSARY Act III

Climax – the high point of a story

Foreshadowing – hinting at future events

Iambic Pentameter – 5 verse feet consisting of an unstressed syllable followed by a stressed one

Irony – when things turn out the opposite of what is expected

Point of View – the vantage point or perspective from which a story is related

Pun – a play on words

Sonnet – 14 lines of iambic pentameter with a fixed rhyme scheme

"ROMEO AND JULIET"
Act III

Principal Conflict(s) #3

In Act III, Romeo intercedes in a fight between Mercutio and Tybalt and indirectly causes Mercutio's fatal injury. As a result, Romeo becomes enraged and kills Tybalt. Therefore, the Prince banishes Romeo. Meanwhile, the Capulets betroth Juliet to Paris, not realizing that she is already wed to Romeo.

Questions for Discussion and Composition:

A **pun** is a play on words. Identify some of the puns uttered by Mercutio as he suffers from the stab wound. Why are they **ironic**?

Act III of a typical Shakespearean play is called the **climax**, which contains a turning point that changes the outcome of the play. Identify which specific event you believe is the turning point.

Some might consider the punishment of banishment lenient. Romeo does not. Explain his perception.

For what reasons do Lord and Lady Capulet wish Juliet to wed Paris?

How would you feel if your parents were authorized to make marital decisions for you?

What causes Lord Capulet to get angry with Juliet? Look at his feelings. Are they comparable to what a parent of today might experience?

Juliet is a teenager created by a writer of the 16th century. What conflicts do teenagers of the 21st century and she have in common despite the difference in time from when the play was written?

Focus Mediation Skills
Act III

Active Listening

In order to truly understand someone, it is important to listen first without speaking or making assumptions of any kind. Most people consider listening to be passive. That is, the listener is receptive. This is partly true. However, to make the best efforts at understanding, it is important to be sure information is heard accurately. This can be accomplished by taking notes while a party is speaking and then reflecting back what was heard to the speaker. Have students break into groups of three to perform the following role plays in front of the class. Have onlookers determine if any pieces of information are misconstrued. Videotaping the process would be helpful if technology is available. Assign one student the role of the mediator, and others to play the various disputants. They need not speak in Elizabethan English but must keep in mind the motives and behaviors of the characters. The mediator must practice active listening by taking notes as the parties speak and then accurately reflecting them back to the speaker. Remember, participants are not to come to any resolution at this point. The objective is to practice the skill of active listening.

Role Play One: Pretend that the fight between Tybalt and Mercutio has been broken up by a citizen of Verona before Romeo enters the scene. The two have been sent to a mediator to explain their sides of the story.

Role Play Two: Pretend that Juliet and her Father have been sent to a mediator to discuss her lack of obedience.

Role Play Three: Pretend that Romeo and Tybalt are sent to a mediator before drawing swords on one another and must discuss the fact that they are now kin.

Role Play Four: Pretend that Juliet and her Mother discuss Juliet's impending marriage to Paris.

Role Play Five: Pretend that Romeo and the Prince see a mediator to discuss the punishment of banishment.

Extended Activities

A. Research the practice of arranged marriages. Where else does this occur? Why? What are some of the intended benefits of this process? Debate the pros and cons.

B. Write the soundtrack for Act III by identifying three songs that are apt, given plot events. Explain your rationale for each selection.

C. Research the role of women during Elizabethan times. How does Juliet compare?

D. Research the median age of marriage during Elizabethan times. Share information with the class. Discuss the possible rationales for this.

E. Write a love letter from Paris to Juliet seeking her hand in marriage. Try to use Elizabethan English.

F. The Shakespearean or Elizabethan **sonnet** is 14 lines of **iambic pentameter** (five verse feet with each foot comprised of an unstressed then stressed syllable). It usually follows the following pattern: ABAB CDCD EFEF GG

G. Have students compose sonnets of their own. Follow just the rhyme scheme for lower level students. Have advanced students use iambic pentameter as well.

Dealing With Conflict QUIZ

Directions: Respond to the following questions in complete sentences explaining your rationale (20 points each):

1. Why does Lady Capulet doubt Benvolio's account of the fight between Tybalt and Mercutio?

2. Whom does Juliet assume is dead when the Nurse first comes to report the news about the latest fight?

3. Why are Juliet's loyalties strained at this point?

4. What ploy does Juliet use to get her father to postpone her wedding?

5. Look at the last lines of this act. What event is possibly being foreshadowed? Explain.

OBJECTIVES Act IV

• Students will increase their knowledge of pertinent literary devices.

• Students will predict the outcome of the play based on inferential material.

• Students will recognize similarities in human behavior, despite setting.

• Students will understand the events leading up to the tragic conclusion of the play.

• Students will practice posing open-ended questions to help disputants think about possible ways of resolving conflict.

GLOSSARY Act IV

Apostrophe – addressing someone or something as if it were present

Character Sketch – a detailed description of the physical and personality traits of a character

Comic Relief – the use of humor after an intense scene

Conflict of interest – double-dealing for the purpose of self-advancement

Metaphor – an implied comparison

Personification – the attribution of human characteristics to non-living things

Simile – a comparison using like or as

"ROMEO AND JULIET"
Act IV

Principal Conflict #4

Friar Laurence comes up with the plan to feign Juliet's death so that she can go away with Romeo.

Questions for Composition and Discussion:

Define **conflict of interest.** What conflicts of interest are faced by Friar Laurence? Are his actions justified? Can you think of any other current events which have involved this issue of conflict of interest?

Explain a difficult decision or ethical conflict that you have faced. What was the outcome? If you could change one thing about this event, what would it be?

What are some of the risks that Juliet assumes by going along with Friar Laurence's plan? (These can be physical or psychological/ to herself or to others). What might likely go wrong?

How do her parents react when they believe that Juliet is dead? What does this show about their underlying feelings?

Shakespeare often used the technique of **comic relief,** which is the insertion of a humorous scene after an intense one. Identify the comic relief in Act IV and analyze its effect on the audience.

Focus Mediation Skill
Act IV

Asking Open-Ended Questions

One of the goals of facilitative mediation is giving power to the disputants to solve their own problems as opposed to determining a solution for them. Disputants are more likely to abide by terms that they have contributed to then to uphold those that are imposed upon them. One technique in helping disputants think about remedies is asking open-ended questions that promote communication and critical thinking. An open-ended question does not simply have a yes/no response.

Step One:
Matching Activity: Read the following scenarios on page 31. Then, examine the open-ended questions to the right and draw a line matching the most appropriate question to elicit the best results from the disputants described on the left. Be prepared to explain your reasoning as well as any possible solutions that might arise from the questions posed.

Conflicts

There is a fight in the cafeteria between two teenaged boys. Nobody is sure who started it or why but there is a rumor throughout the school that they plan to continue fighting after school.

A 15-year old girl has run away from home. She has no place to go but is angry with her parents and refuses to return with them.

A mother is so angry at her disobedient daughter that she ripped up her prom tickets and grounded the girl as to keep her from attending the event and teach her a lesson.

Questions

What might happen if you do not find a way to resolve this problem?

How would you like to see this resolved?

How does that make you feel?

Focus Mediations Skills
Act IV Continued

Teacher's Notes: In actuality, any of the questions would work with any of the given scenarios in the matching activity. However, answers will vary on the possible responses they may elicit.

Step Two: Reassign the role plays from Act III on page 23. Be sure that there are different students mediating so as many participants as possible have an opportunity to practice. In addition to active listening, mediators should now pose open-ended questions to the disputants after each side is told. Students may use some of the questions from the matching exercise but are encouraged to try some of their own. If there are enough students in the class, it is helpful to have one observer who can take notes on the process and give a report after the activity about which questions worked well and which ones did not.

Step Three (optional): The above activity can be done multiple times by having students change roles. During the process, students should keep journals documenting their successes and failures as mediators, their feelings while playing a disputant, any questions or suggestions they might want to discuss, as well as observations in general. This information should be shared in a debriefing session. Teachers may opt to grade journals as well.

Extended Activities

A. If you were in Juliet's position, would you have acted in the same manner? What are some of the other options for handling this conflict? Make a flow chart to represent these ideas.

B. Break students into groups. Have them predict the outcome of the play and write a brief script to this end. Act out the alternate endings.

C. Have students design a playbill or poster for the play. Points should be given for demonstration of understanding of purpose, target audience, originality, and graphics.

D. Research "Tristan and Isolde" and "Pyramus and Thisbe." Compare these and any other stories of "star crossed lovers" with which students might be familiar to "Romeo and Juliet." Why is this concept still popular today?

E. Have students select a favorite character and write a **character sketch** for that person. Watch the Franco Zeferelli movie version of the play. Does this director's interpretation align with the students' descriptions? Discuss.

Dealing With Conflict QUIZ

Directions: Respond to the following questions in complete sentences explaining your rationale (20 points each):

1. What excuse does Juliet use as a reason for visiting Friar Laurence?

2. To what city has Romeo been banished?

3. How will Romeo be informed of the plan?

4. Identify the literary device demonstrated in the following line – "Death lies on her like an untimely frost."

5. Identify the literary device in the following lines – "Death is my heir;/My daughter he hath wedded."

OBJECTIVES Act V

- Students will examine the consequences of unresolved conflict.

- Students will increase knowledge and application of literary terms.

- Students can complete a mock mediation.

- Students increase understanding of the play as a whole.

GLOSSARY Act V

Allusion – a reference to something outside of the text which is commonly known

Anachronism – the existence of something outside of its proper time frame

Comedy – a play in which the outcome is happy (not funny!)

Soliloquy – a monologue delivered when a character is alone so that the audience may overhear his/her thoughts

Tragedy – a play in which the outcome is of doom and usually all of the principal characters are dead

"ROMEO AND JULIET"
Act V

Principal Conflict #5

Romeo never gets word of Friar Laurence's plan. He hears the false report that Juliet is dead and returns to Verona. Upon seeing what he believes to be her corpse, he kills himself. Immediately afterward, Juliet awakens. She sees Romeo's dead body and kills herself out of grief.

Questions for Composition and Discussion:

What motivates the apothecary to give the drugs to Romeo despite the severe penalty for doing so? What are some common reasons that people break the law? Is it ever acceptable to break the law?

Does Romeo really need to kill Paris? Why does he do it? List some of the emotions he may have been feeling at the time. How could he better have handled the situation?

Many people are grief-stricken at the conclusion of this play. What are some of the negative effects of this grief? What are some of the positive results? Can you think of any cases where this is so in real life?

Who is most at fault for the tragic events of the play? Is blame helpful at this point?

Select one of the famous lines from the play as a whole listed below for interpretation:

"He jests at scars that never felt the wound." (Romeo 2.2.1)

"What's in a name? That which we call a rose/By any other word would smell as sweet." (Juliet 2.2.43-44)

"For never was a story of more woe/Than this of Juliet and her Romeo." (Prince 5,3,309-31)

Extended Activities

A. An **allusion** is a reference to something outside of the play. There are many mythological allusions in this work. Have students go back through the play and find five of them. Identify them and explain how they contribute to the meaning of the lines in which they are found.

B. Have students rewrite the conclusion of the play so that it is a **romantic comedy**, not a **tragedy**.

C. Have the class watch the modern version of this play featuring Leonardo DiCaprio. Compare it to the older version and the original play itself. Identify as many **anachronisms** as possible. What comment might this make about changes in society since Elizabethan times?

(D) In understanding conflict, understanding a party's key issues, assumptions, perspectives, and emotions is important. This can be better achieved by having a precise understanding of language. Assign one of the **soliloquies** to be translated as closely as possible into modern text.

Dealing With Conflict QUIZ

Directions: Respond to the following questions in complete sentences explaining your rationale (20 points each):

1. How do Romeo's rash actions further the tragic ending of the play?

2. If you were a prosecuting attorney, would you hold Balthasar responsible for the tragic events of the play?

3. If you were a defense attorney, how would you defend Balthasar?

4. Should the Prince punish Balthasar for his involvement in the tragic events of the play? If so, why and how?

5. Do you think that there will be a longstanding peace in Verona now? Support your claim.

Final Assessments

Mock Mediation

Directions:. Have students conduct role-play mediations from start to finish in front of the class or as group work. Remind students of the overall mediation process from the beginning of this unit. (Simply stated, a mediator is a neutral third party who helps facilitate communication between two or more disputants.) Place students in groups of three. Assign the roles of Mediator, Old Capulet, and Old Montague. Capulet and Montague may ad lib as needed; for example, the reader never knows exactly how the fray begins. However, students do know what it is like to feel angry and to adopt positions from which it is difficult to move and can act accordingly. Provide students some time to think how these characters would actually feel and react before beginning. If necessary, provide a summary of issues for those who need assistance.

If done in front of the class, have onlookers note things like body language of parties, active listening, questions/behaviors that were helpful, questions/behaviors that were not, etc. If done in small groups run simultaneously, ask a fourth student to observe the mediation and record the process and outcome to report back to the class at its conclusion. Also, as a final product, the mediator should write up an agreement if one is reached. The best agreements are fair and equal. That is, each party is responsible for some part of it. Also, it is written in neutral language. Use the format below or have students come up with their own document.

It is hereby noted that on this day of_____, Old Capulet and Old Montague have agreed to the following terms:

Signatures:

Final Assessments Continued

Paper

Directions: Compose a five paragraph paper in which you respond to the prompt below. Be sure to embed any quotations from "Romeo and Juliet" properly. All papers must be typed in 12 point font. Do your pre-writing at the bottom of this page. Due date:_____

Point Distribution:

Clear thesis – 10 points
Organization – 20 points
Mechanics –20 points
Analysis – 30 points
Textural Evidence – 20 points

If you were a court-appointed mediator assigned to resolve the conflicts of Verona, how would you direct the process? Which disputants would you address first and why? What sorts of questions would you ask and what information would you hope to gain. Are there any other strategies you would employ? Given the description of characters, what likely responses would you receive? Use examples from the text to support your assertions.

Conflict Resolution Through Literature